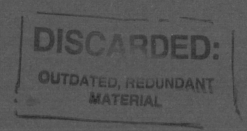

Animals That Make Me Say Look Out!

Ranger Rick®

Animals That Make Me Say Look Out!

Ranger Rick®

Dawn Cusick

imagine!
Publishing

Copyright © 2016 by Charlesbridge Publishing, Inc.
Image copyrights held by the photographers on page 79
Text Copyright © 2016 by Dawn Cusick

An Imagine Book
Published by Charlesbridge
85 Main Street, Watertown, MA 02472
(617) 926-0329
www.charlesbridge.com

Library of Congress Cataloging-in-Publication Data
is available upon request.

ISBN 978-1-62354-080-7 (reinforced for library use)
ISBN 978-1-60734-965-5 (ebook)
ISBN 978-1-60734-966-2 (ebook pdf)

Printed in China. Manufactured in March 2016.

(hc) 10 9 8 7 6 5 4 3 2 1

Display type and text type set in Motter Corpus and Frutiger.

Jacket and Type Design: Megan Kirby
Proofreading: Meredith Hale
Produced by EarlyLight Books

Contents

Florida panther

Introduction

In the animal world, we often need to say look out!

When we see animals defending themselves in wild ways, it can make us say look out. Mandrills and otters show their sharp teeth as threats. Some spiders and snakes camouflage themselves so well that we are shocked and surprised when we finally notice them. Animals such as frogs, beetles, and opossums confuse predators (and people!) by playing dead.

We also need to look out for ways we can protect animals and the places they live. Many wild cats, bats, and amphibians have lost a lot of habitat because of human building and pollution. Other animals are in trouble because invasive animals have moved in to new places, taking food and space from local animals.

There's a lot to learn, so start reading!

crocodiles

LOOK OUT

FOR ANIMALS ON THE DEFENSE

In the natural world, animals can look and behave in ways you would not expect. From poison and venom to camouflage and scary stares, check out the wild things animals do to defend themselves.

tiger shark

Take a Deep Breath Before You Panic

Getting enough oxygen across their gills is important for all fish. Some sharks use a process called ram ventilation to get extra oxygen. To do this, they swim fast with their mouths open. So if you're diving or snorkeling in the ocean and see a shark underwater with a wide-open mouth headed your way, you may not need to worry. If you're on top of the water and see an open-mouthed tiger shark headed your way, it might be time to say look out!

tiger shark

My, What Big Teeth You Have!

Crocodiles and alligators often rest with their mouths wide open. This behavior is called gaping. Gaping may also serve as a threat, showing the size of jaws and teeth to rivals.

alligator

Gaping, Not Yawning

Crocodiles and alligators also use gaping to lower their body temperatures. As ectotherms, they need the sun's energy for heat. Ectotherms are animals that need outside heat sources such as the sun to warm their bodies.

alligator

mandrill

You've Been Warned!

Many animals open their mouths to show their sharp teeth and wide jaws when they feel threatened or when they want to threaten another animal. These warning signals may save animals from wasting energy on fighting and risking getting hurt.

lizard

giant river otter

hippopotamus

Not All Tusks Are the Same

walrus

Not all tusks come from the same types of teeth. The warthog's upper tusks grow from canine teeth, as walrus tusks do. (Canine teeth are the longer, pointed teeth found in pairs, one pair on the top and one on the bottom.) Warthogs also have lower tusks that grow from lower canine teeth. Elephant tusks grow from their top front teeth (called incisors).

warthog

Animals use their tusks for different tasks. Walruses use their tusks to help them move on land, and males use them as fighting tools. Warthogs use their tusks to protect them-selves from predators. Male warthogs also use them to fight for females. Elephants use their tusks as tools to help them get food. Males also use them in fights.

Animal tusks can differ from place to place. For example, female elephants from India do not have tusks, and walruses from the Arctic have much longer tusks than walruses that live in other places do. Longer tusks may help Arctic walruses move on the ice.

African elephant

walrus

Imagine Brushing These Teeth!

What do you call a walrus's two large canine teeth? Tusks! Walrus tusks keep growing for the animal's entire life. Some walruses have tusks that are several feet long! Both males and females have tusks, but male tusks are usually longer.

walrus

walrus

World Record Holder

The box jellyfish from Australia is Earth's most venomous ocean animal. Its strong venom quickly acts on prey.

box jellies

Blue Means Look Out!

How do you know when the blue-ringed octopus is upset? Look for blue rings!

Blue-ringed octopuses have enough venom to kill several people. They have two types of venom. One type helps them catch prey such as crabs and shrimp. The other type protects them from predators.

blue-ringed octopus

Fast, Fierce Bites

Look out! Taipans have one of the most toxic snake venoms in the world. They also use a "snap-and-release" biting style that lets them bite large prey many times very quickly.

Taipans live in Australia, New Zealand, and New Guinea. They prey on lizards, birds, and small mammals such as rats or marsupials known as bandicoots.

taipan snake

taipan

LOOK OUT
FOR ANIMALS ON THE DEFENSE
VENOM & POISON

Strong Venom

Brazilian wandering spiders are one of the most venomous spiders in the world. They use their venom to defend themselves and to kill prey such as insects, small mammals, and reptiles.

wandering spider

scorpion

Tail-Tip Venom

A scorpion stores its venom in a sac at the tip of its tail. The stinger that delivers the venom is super sharp, like a doctor's needle. The venom protects scorpions from predators and stuns or kills prey.

Toxic Mucus

Poison dart frogs release strong toxins in the mucus that keeps their skin moist. Where do poison frogs get their toxins? Probably from the insects they eat. The insects may get these toxins from the rainforest plants they eat. Bright skin colors warn other animals that these frogs are poisonous.

Venom vs. Poison

Venoms are injected with bites or stings, while poisons are ingested.

poison dart frog

bear

Charge!

A charging bear has its head down and runs fast on all four legs. A bear can also "bluff charge," which means it will stop at the last minute.

Slow, Quiet Steps

Predators that are about to attack often lower their body and crouch to hide from prey. Large wild cats such as this jaguar often take many quiet steps toward their prey before chasing them at top speed. This type of behavior is called stalking.

jaguar

Indian rhinoceros

boar

Staring Contests

In the animal world, staring contests are not fun and games. Direct stares are a sign of aggression. When a direct stare comes with a lowered head, look out! A pounce or a charge may be close behind.

Stand Back, Jack

You probably already know that crocodiles are strong swimmers. Did you know they can also use their tails and back feet to push their bodies upward straight up and out of the water?

crocodiles

No Laughing Matter

Of course you would take a charging lion seriously, but what would you do if a swan were charging you? Like many other types of birds, swans attack to defend their eggs and chicks. Birds spend a lot of time protecting their nests from predators such as other birds, raccoons, and snakes.

duck

gull

swan

mantis

The Eyes Have It!

Some animals such as this mantis have colorations called eyespots that looks like large eyes. When threatened, they spread out their legs and wings, tricking predators into thinking they are larger and more dangerous than they are.

mantis

tarantula

Threat Displays Say, "Look Out!"

When they feel threatened by a predator or another animal that invades their territory, many animals try to look larger. They may stand up taller, lift up their tails, open their jaws, or spread out their front limbs. If you see an animal giving a threat display, leave it alone.

LOOK OUT

FOR ANIMALS ON THE DEFENSE

gecko

beetle

crayfish

LOOK OUT

FOR ANIMALS ON THE DEFENSE

PREDATORS & PREY

lion

Water With Dinner?

Water holes and rivers are favorite hunting places for sit-and-wait predators such as lions and crocodiles. Many prey animals visit water holes in groups. Traveling in a group means there are more eyes to spot predators and less chance of being caught.

African animals

crocodile & wildebeests

Where's Mom When You Need Her?

Reptiles, fish, mammals, and other birds prey on ducklings when they stray from their parents.

Safe Travels

Some aquatic birds forage for fish with their hatchlings riding on their backs. As the hatchlings become better swimmers, they will start traveling behind the parent instead of on top of it.

duckling & water snake

female common merganser & chicks

Beat It, Buddy

Squirrels defend their tree holes with claws and teeth. The holes are more than just resting spots. They serve as nests for newborns and safe places to store nuts.

squirrels

Learning from Fights

Many animals of the same kind fight for homes, food, and mates. Even though these animals fight fiercely with defense tools, the losers usually do not get injured. Animals may use sharp teeth, claws, and horns to find out how strong their opponent is. If an animal thinks it will lose the fight, it may back off.

tigers

bison

Food Fight!

It can be tough work finding and catching a meal, so some birds may take food from other birds. It takes a lot of energy to steal from others, though, so they cannot afford to lose many food fights.

gull & pelican

cormorants & heron

Strength in Numbers

One coyote can easily chase away a single crow or raven scavenging at a carcass. The birds gain the advantage in numbers, mobbing the lone mammal for their place at the dinner table.

crows

coyote

hognose snake

Great Pretenders

Eastern hognose snakes pretend they are dead to confuse predators such as opossums, foxes, owls, hawks, and other snakes. When playing dead, the snake rolls over, opens its mouth, sometimes lets its tongue hang out, and emits a foul smell that tricks predators into thinking it's already dead and rotting. The hognose snake's predators do not like to eat carrion (dead animals).

The eastern hognose snake can also fool predators another way. It flattens its neck and hisses, the way venomous cobra snakes do.

hognose snake

Playing Possum

Opossums are so good at playing dead that the behavior was named after them! To play dead, an opossum rolls on its side and drools. Sometimes it will even defecate (poop). The opossum can play dead for a few minutes or several hours. If it feels threatened again, the opossum will fall to the ground and play dead again.

opossum

ring-neck snake

ring-neck snake

Double Trouble

Ring-neck snakes fool predators in two ways. When threatened, they play dead by rolling over and curling up their tails. Bright yellow and red colors on their undersides mimic the colors of animals with toxins.

flower
chafer
beetle

Beetle Actors

There are more than 350,000 types of beetles, and many of them play dead. Notice how this beetle has tucked its front and back legs close to its body.

Scamming Spiders

Wouldn't it be dangerous to play dead when a predator is close on your heels? Not if you are a snout beetle and your spider predator prefers live prey!

snout beetle

spider

Toad and Frog Fakers

Some toads and frogs play dead to confuse predators. Like other animals, they have to decide very fast whether to try escaping or whether to play dead. Some frogs and toads have another defense: puffing themselves up to look larger than they are. How do toads and frogs make such important decisions so quickly? Special cells in their bodies called neurons send information to their brains very fast. You have neurons that help you act fast when you're in danger, too.

Spiders Play Dead, Too

A spider that plays dead may fool predators, but do not let it fool you.

toad

underwing moth

katydid

Blending In

Birds that feed on insects use their great eyesight to help them search. Insects that look like tree bark or leaves may be able to fool hunting birds.

oak leaf butterfly

LOOK OUT

CAMOUFLAGE

leaf insect

Sit Still!

Many insects are perfectly camouflaged on plants because the veins in their wings look a lot like the veins in leaves.

Even if animals look exactly like a leaf or a branch, it can still be hard to fool predators. Many predators find prey by searching for small movements. Check out the animals to the right and below. Would they be easier to find if they were moving?

moss frog

leaf insect

gray tree frog

wrap-around spider

Curiosity Killed the Fish

Most frogfish blend in well with their backgrounds, which helps them trick their prey. Instead of hunting down food, frogfish attract prey with a body part that looks like a wiggling worm or fish. When a curious fish comes over for what looks like a tasty treat, the frogfish sucks it in!

Paddle Walkers

Frogfish use two types of fins to walk across ocean floors. They have lumpy, loose-fitting skin, and can make themselves look bigger to predators by filling their stomachs with air or water.

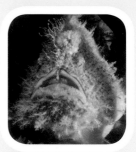

frogfish

frogfish

bearded scorpionfish

Now You See Me . . .

Scorpionfish blend in well with coral reefs and ocean floors. Camouflage helps them hide from predators such as snapper fish, eels, sharks, and rays.

tasseled scorpionfish

Camouflaging Fins and Spines

Scorpionfish use venom-filled spines to protect themselves from some predators. The spines do not protect them from humans, though, as people still carefully take scorpionfish from the wild and sell them for pets.

Hide-and-Seek

The desert horned viper uses sand to keep cool during hot days. To get its body under sand, the snake moves quickly from side to side. The desert horned viper usually hunts small mammals, lizards, and insects at night, but if these animals come too close to a camouflaged snake during the day, the viper will strike. This snake is venomous, and lives in North Africa and the Middle East.

desert horned viper

desert horned viper

LOOK OUT

FOR ANIMALS ON THE DEFENSE

CAMOUFLAGE

Tree Vines

Green-striped vine snakes live in rain forests in South America. They hide from ground predators in trees, coiled up like vines. How long did it take you to notice the snake's head in this photo?

vine snake

copperhead snake

Copperhead Camouflage

Copperhead snake scales come in many shades of brown. These colors help copperheads blend in with leaf litter on forest floors. Their camouflage helps copperheads be good ambush predators. Some prey do not see them until it's too late. It also hides the snakes from predators.

LOOK OUT

FOR ANIMALS ON THE DEFENSE

CAMOUFLAGE

Blending Birds

Many young birds and adult females blend in well with tree branches and bark to help them hide from predators.

ruffed grouse

tawny owl

Hiding Sloths

How would you hide if your biggest predator were one of the largest eagles in the world? South American harpy eagles search for prey as they fly over tree canopies. Their talons are long and strong enough to pull monkeys and sloths from the trees. For sloths, hanging upside down helps them hide from the hungry eagles above.

harpy eagle

two-toed sloth

spider
monkey

Trustworthy Tails

Hanging upside down high up in a tree might feel scary to you and me. For many primates, though, their super-strong tails work as extra limbs, allowing them to reach more food. These types of tails are called pre-hensile (pree-hen-sul). The undersides of many prehensile tails have less fur, which helps them get better grips.

vervet monkey

howler monkeys

tree frog

Safety First!

Spending your sleep time high up in trees makes sense when there are so many predators on the ground. Sleeping upside down makes sense when your ankles and knees face backward, an adaptation that helps bats with flight. More than 20 percent of all mammal species are bats.

flying fox

Toe Pads

Tree frogs use a combination of sticky mucus and flat toe tips to climb and cling to surfaces. They do not have webbing between their toes, the way aquatic frogs do.

parrot

Climbing Feet

Parrots spend a lot of time climbing trees and limbs and hanging upside down. The bones in their feet help them do this. Two toes face forward and two face backward. (Look at your toes. Do they all face the same direction?) Some parrots also use their strong feet to hold nuts and fruits.

Cuckoos, woodpeckers, mousebirds, and some owls and swifts also have toes that face both ways: forward and backward.

Lots of Legs!

Caterpillars have three pairs of true legs in the front of their bodies. They also have extra pairs of legs (called prolegs) that adult insects do not have. Caterpillars can hang upside down to feed and hide because there are small hooks in their prolegs that grip twigs and leaves.

caterpillar

burrowing owls

LOOK OUT

FOR WAYS TO PROTECT ANIMALS

Animals need our protection for many reasons. The habitats and ecosystems they live in also need our protection. The more you learn, the more you will be able to help.

Safe Crossings

Mountain lions in California's Los Angeles Santa Monica mountains often must cross freeways to get from place to place. Sadly, growing numbers of these cats are killed by oncoming cars and trucks. In one dangerous place, National Wildlife Federation is helping to build an overpass so the animals can cross safely. It may become the largest wildlife crossing in the world.

mountain lion

Florida panther

Look Out for Poisons

Poisons used to hurt one type of animal often end up hurting other animals as well. Bobcats are a good example. These small wild cats live in North America. They often feed on rodents such as rats. If they eat rats that have been poisoned by people, they can get very sick and may die.

bobcat

bobcat

Animal Math

Florida panthers need a lot of space. The almost 20 million people who live in the state of Florida also need a lot of space. So do their 19 million cars. The more than 80 million people who visit Florida every year need a lot of space, too.

The Florida panther has a large hunting range. Each male needs almost 200 square miles! There are about 150 Florida panthers left in the wild. To help protect them from cars while traveling, Florida has built fences along busy roads and tunnels that go under roads.

frog

Food for Many

Most types of frogs lay thousands and thousands of eggs, but only a few eggs become adult frogs. Frog eggs (called spawn) have many predators, including fish, snakes, snails, and even water molds. Tadpoles that hatch from eggs are food for other types of animals.

frog eggs

Frog Futures?

We like to look at frogs and talk about frogs, but do we want to save frogs? Many of the world's frogs and other amphibians may go extinct if we don't work to protect them.

Diseases have killed many frogs. Many other frogs are threatened because humans have destroyed frog habitats with pollution or building.

poison
dart frogs

Frog Food

If the number of frogs keeps going down, the animals that feed on frogs will have problems, too. Birds, snakes, spiders, and many other animals feed on frogs.

toad

burrowing owls

Unsafe Ground

These small owls lay their eggs and raise their chicks in burrows instead of in tree nests. When humans build houses and roads in burrowing owl habitat, many owls and other animals lose their homes. Floods have also caused problems for burrowing owls.

burrowing owls

Low Numbers

Burrowing owls used to live all over western North America. Now they live in fewer places, and every year there are fewer of them. Even though they lay more eggs than most tree-nesting birds, most of their eggs and chicks do not survive to become adults.

owls

pelicans

brown pelican

Clean Water Needed

Pelicans may look like they're on vacation every day. They live on ocean coastlines and rivers around the world and spend most of their time hunting for fish.

Pelicans face many problems caused by humans, though. Pelicans use their feathers to stay warm and for flight, and oil spills can ruin their feathers. When farm chemicals run into the water, they move up the food chain and into pelicans, causing their egg shells to be weak and easily cracked.

humpback whale

Protection Helps

Many whale species, such as humpback whales, were pushed to the brink of extinction by overhunting by humans. Luckily, whales are now protected in much of the world and their numbers are growing.

Troubled Times

About 325 species of turtles and tortoises live around the world, and about 75 percent of these species are in trouble. In some parts of the world, humans kill turtles for food or medicine, or steal them from the wild to become pets. Humans have also damaged many turtle habitats.

alligator snapping turtle

Take Care

Aquatic and marine turtles that live in places where people fish can get caught up in fishing lines. Trash from humans such as plastic bags also causes problems for turtles. Turtles may eat the trash and become sick, or get tangled in it, wounding or drowning them.

loggerhead

Small Homes, Small Populations

When animals live in only one place, such as a single rain forest or just one island, we have to work harder to protect them. These animals can be hurt by floods, fires, hunting, and diseases.

tarsier

cotton-top tamarin

Tamarin Tragedy

These South American primates are critically endangered. Their forest habitat is quickly disappearing. People cut down forests to make money on lumber and make room for roads and houses.

brown bat

Winter Sleep

Finding safe places for winter hibernation is a problem for many bats. It can also be hard for them to find enough food to get the body fat they need to make it through the winter.

fruit bat

Important Work

Bats are important parts of many ecosystems. Some bats pollinate flowers and some spread plant seeds. Other bats eat disease-causing and crop-destroying pest insects.

flying fox

Flying Mammals

There are about 1,000 species (types) of bats, and about one out of every four mammals is a bat. Many bat species are in trouble, though. In some parts of the world, people eat bats. In other places, humans have taken away their habitats. In North America, millions of bats have died from a new fungal infection called white-nose syndrome.

northern long-eared bat

Low Numbers

Most West Indian manatees live along coastlines in parts of Florida, South America, and the Caribbean. These large herbivores, which are related to elephants, spend most of their time searching for food. With fewer than 4,000 manatees left in the United States, the "sea cow" is an endangered species. Boating accidents injure and kill many manatees a year. Fishing hooks and crab nets also cause problems for manatees. The number of manatees will continue to go down unless people do more to make their habitats safe.

manatee

Manatee Moms

Like most large mammals, manatee moms spend a lot of time taking care of their young. Usually, females only have one calf at a time.

manatees

Monk Seals

As a species gets closer to extinction, its numbers start to get smaller and smaller. There are only about 1,100 Hawaiian monk seals left in the world, and there are fewer of them every year. Some seals get caught in fishing lines and nets, and big fishing companies have caused declines in the monk seal's prey.

Hawaiian monk seal

pika

Pika Problems

Related to rabbits and hares, American pikas live high up in the cool mountains of many western states. As temperatures have become warmer with global climate change, pikas have disappeared from several of the places they used to live.

With the help of funds from National Wildlife Federation, leading pika scientists are collecting data and studying how climate change impacts these pikas.

Winter Coats

Pikas do not hibernate during cold winters. Instead, their super-warm fur keeps them warm. These warm coats can cause pikas to overheat during hot summers. To avoid the heat, pikas can spend parts of the day underground, where it's cooler. But too much time underground may leave pikas with too little time to find food.

pika

cowbird

No Time for Nests

Cowbirds were named for their habit of hanging around with bison and cows. Why did they hang out with the big grazers? Free food! As the herd walked along, insects flew up from the grass, and cowbirds grabbed an easy meal.

Because they traveled with these herds that were always on the move, female cowbirds left their eggs in the nests of foster parents instead of building their own nests.

bison with cowbirds

cardinal feeding
cowbird chick

What Big Wings You Have!

The foster parents are usually songbirds. Cowbird eggs are often larger than the songbird eggs. They usually hatch sooner, too, and grow faster than the nest owner's chicks. In some species, the nest owner knows the wrong egg is in its nest and tosses it out. In other species, the nest parents take care of the cowbird eggs and chicks.

While cowbirds impact local songbird populations, habitat loss and climate change are the big reasons there are fewer songbirds now than there were a few hundred years ago.

crown-of-thorns sea star

Beauty or Beast?

Colorful spines may make the crown-of-thorns sea star look cool. Dozens of sharp, venomous spines make it look fierce. These sea stars feed on coral on Australia's Great Barrier Reef. When they eat fast-growing coral, they help coral ecosystems by giving slow-growing corals a chance to grow. Also, large groups of these sea stars sometimes eat so much coral that they destroy a reef. Crown-of-thorn sea stars can eat more than 12 miles of coral reef each year.

LOOK OUT

FOR WAYS TO PROTECT ANIMALS

INVASIVE SPECIES

Scary Snakeheads

In Asia, northern snakehead fish are just another part of the ecosystem. In North America, this invasive species is causing a lot of damage. The snakeheads prey on native fish, and they also eat many of the same foods native fish eat. With lots of food and few predators, the number of snakeheads in American rivers may only increase.

snake-head

Far From Home

Did northern snakeheads swim from Asia to North America? Nope. Like many invasive species, snakeheads were brought to North America by people. Some snakeheads were brought over for pet stores, while others were brought for restaurants.

Asian carp

Carp Trouble

Carp from Asia are also found in many North American waters. These large fish cause many of the same problems that snakehead fish cause. In the photo here, the US Fish and Wildlife Service works to stop invasive carp from spreading.

lionfish

Two Million Eggs and Counting . . .

What happens when pet owners release home aquarium fish into nearby oceans? Some of them, such as the lionfish of Indonesia, become invasive and out-compete native fish. Native fish in North American waters cannot defend themselves against the lionfish's venomous spines. Female lionfish can lay a million eggs twice a year.

lionfish

Unwelcome Visitors

With strong ocean currents or ballast water from cargo ships, jellyfish eggs and newly hatched larvae can travel from one part of the world to another. Jellyfish can reproduce very quickly in their new habitats if water temperature and food conditions are just right.

The Australian spotted jellyfish (below) has invaded the Gulf of Mexico. Each jellyfish can eat several thousand fish eggs every day. They also feed on the plankton that native species need to eat to survive.

zebra mussels

Expensive Hitchhikers

The United States Coast Guard spends thousands of hours and millions of dollars every year removing invasive zebra mussels from the Great Lakes, ocean coastlines, and small rivers.

Like many other invasive species, zebra mussels feed on plankton, which takes food away from native animals.

spotted jellyfish

wolves

TV Shows & Movies Aren't Always True . . .

Even though people know that many of the wolf stories they see on TV and in the movies are fiction, they may still believe bad things about wolves. Wolves spend a lot of time searching for food and taking care of their young. They avoid humans as much as possible.

wolves

Balance of Nature

When ecosystems are missing a top predator, the numbers of herbivores (plant-eating animals) such as deer and elk can go up. Too many large herbivores means less food for small herbivores, such as rabbits.

Thanks for Dinner!

Biologists who studied wolves in Yellowstone National Park learned that bears, eagles, wolverines, foxes, and ravens feed on the carcasses of wolf prey. Having wolves in Yellowstone helps all of these other animals find a meal.

A+ Students

Raccoons are fast learners and have great memories, too. They can remember many of the things they learn for three years!

raccoon

raccoons

No Way!

Biologists wondered whether animals that live in the city have bigger brains. When the scientists tested brain sizes in bats, mice, gophers, voles, shrews, and squirrels, they found that city brains were larger than country brains. City raccoons may also have larger brains. These larger brain sizes may help deal with city problems such as cars, finding natural foods, and more.

mouse

raccoon

coyotes

Feeding Pups

Both coyote parents protect and feed their pups. Moms feed young pups with milk. Dads bring food to nursing moms. Both parents also vomit up food for older pups. Sometimes other pack members vomit up food for pups, too.

coyotes

City Living

Can coyotes really live in big cities? Yes, they can! Many wild animals cannot survive in big cities because they cannot find the right kinds of food, or they're hit by cars. Coyotes are not picky eaters, and most of them are smart enough to stay away from moving cars and people.

coyote

Home, Sweet Home

Biologists have been studying coyotes in Chicago for more than fifteen years. They found that some coyotes travel more than fifty miles each night. About 2,000 coyotes live in Chicago. Coyotes also live in other big American cities such as New York and Washington, DC.

Coyotes live in many kinds of rural habitats, too, including deserts, forests, and prairies in North and Central America.

SCAVENGER HUNT CHALLENGES

green anole

Many animals hide to protect themselves from hungry predators. The animal hiding here is a green anole. **SCAVENGER HUNT CHALLENGE:** Find a quiet place outside to sit down for at least twenty minutes. Bring a pen and write down every animal you see. Put a star next to every animal that was hiding. Did you find more animals at the beginning or at the end of your observation time? Remember that insects, spiders, and earthworms are animals, too!

hippopotamuses

Young animals may look cute, but it's not a good idea to get close to them. A female hippo will fight lions, crocodiles, leopards, hyenas, and even people if she believes her calf is in danger. **SCAVENGER HUNT CHALLENGE:** Make a list of your four favorite mammals. Do a web search for how these parents protect their young from predators.

SCAVENGER HUNT CHALLENGES

horned grebes

Young water birds know how to swim and find food without practice because of their genes. They learn how to do these things better, though, by watching their parents. **SCAVENGER HUNT CHALLENGES:** Inside, do a video search for "ducklings learning to swim." Outside, spend an hour watching at least five moving animals as they swim, fly, or run. How often do they change directions or stop and rest?

mongoose & ground squirrel

Ground holes offer protection from predators and the weather, but they are not perfect homes. Carnivores such as the mongoose (at left) can use their strong sense of smell to find prey. **SCAVENGER HUNT CHALLENGES:** How many animals can you name that live in ground holes? How do their predators find prey?

READ MORE

FROM THE NATIONAL WILDLIFE FEDERATION:

FUN ON THE WEB:
RangerRick.com for a world of kids' fun.

MAGAZINES:

OTHER BOOKS IN THE SERIES:

ANIMALS THAT MAKE ME SAY EWWW! by Dawn Cusick;
     Imagine/Charlesbridge (2016).

ANIMALS THAT MAKE ME SAY WOW! by Dawn Cusick;
     Imagine/Charlesbridge (2014).

ANIMALS THAT MAKE ME SAY OUCH! by Dawn Cusick;
     Imagine/Charlesbridge (2014).

OTHER BOOKS FROM THE AUTHOR:

GET THE SCOOP ON ANIMAL PUKE!;
     Imagine/Charlesbridge (2014).

GET THE SCOOP ON ANIMAL POOP!;
     Imagine/Charlesbridge (2012).

ANIMAL SNACKS;
     EarlyLight Books (2012).

ANIMAL EGGS;
     EarlyLight Books (2012).

COOL ANIMAL NAMES;
     Imagine/Charlesbridge (2011).

Adaptation: A change in an organism's behavior or form that helps it fit in better with its environment.

Ballast water: The water in the bottom of cargo ships that helps keep ships level.

Behavior: The way organisms act.

Camouflage: To blend in with the environment.

Carnivore: An animal that eats other animals.

Communication: The sharing of information. Some organisms communicate with sounds or movements, while others communicate with colors or chemicals.

Ecosystem: The living and nonliving parts of an environment functioning together.

Evolve: To change over time in ways that help organisms compete for resources such as food, habitat, mates, and avoiding predators.

Habitat: The home for an organism or a group of organisms.

Hatchling: An animal that has recently hatched from an egg.

Herbivore: An animal that eats plants.

Larva/Larvae (singular/plural): The worm-like, wingless stage of some types of newly hatched insects.

Plankton: The group of living and non-living things that float on the surface of large bodies of water. Plankton is the foundation of the world's food chain, and contains a lot of eggs, seeds, and algae.

Population: A group of organisms from the same species that live together.

Predator: An organism that preys on other organisms.

Prey: An animal being hunted or eaten by another animal.

Territory: An area that an organism lives in and defends.

Toxin: A poisonous substance produced by organisms to help defend themselves from predators or to help them kill prey.

Venom: Poison used by an organism as part of its defense or to find food that is moved through a bite or a sting.

Musk-oxen live in groups in parts of the Arctic. When they feel threatened, they move into a circle with their heads facing outward and their calves in the middle.

musk-oxen

RESEARCH

The author would like to thank and acknowledge the following scientists, organizations, and institutions for their research assistance.

From the National Wildlife Federation:

Mary Dalheim, Kathy Kranking, Ellen Lambeth, Hannah Schardt, Deana Duffek, Michael Morris, Kristen Ferriere, the entire Ranger Rick publication staff, and NWF Naturalist David Mizejewski

From Other Sources:

Jeanette Coy Acevich, Mehdi Adjeroud, Amphibian and Reptile Diversity Center/University of Texas-Austin, Genny Anderson, Kurt A. Anderson, Animal Diversity Web/University of Michigan, Australian Museum, Ammar Aziz, Bat Conservation International, William Bates, BioKIDS, Pauline Bosserelle, Diane L. Brinkman, M.A. Britton, Yannick Chancerelle, E. Charpentier, Colorado Department of Natural Resources, John M. Coluccy, Stacey A. Combes, The Cornell Lab of Ornithology, Zeke Davidson, Sophie DeLaCour, Christine Dell'Amore, Thierry Lison de Loma, David S. Dobkin, Ducks Unlimited, J.E. Earl, Ecological and Water Resources/Minnesota Department of Natural Resources, Paul R. Ehrlich, Florida Department of Transportation, Florida Fish and Wildlife Conservation Commission, Florida Museum of Natural History, Michael Fogden, Patricia Fogden, Caroline Fraser, Sylvie Geoffroy, Stanley Gerht, Kenneth E. Goehring, M.J. Gray, Great Barrier Reef Marine Park Authority/Australian Government, Harry W. Greene, IUCN Conservation Centre, Jordan Johnson, Mohsen Kayal, L.A. Knapp, S.R. Leigh, Jacqueline D. Litzgus, Alex Loukas, Marine Education Society of Australasia, Marine Resources Council, Cody P. Massing, Clinton Hart Merriam, Metropolitan Oceanic Institute & Aquarium, François Michonneau, Constance I. Millar, Takahisa Miyatake, Jason Mulvenna, National Invasive Species Information Center/United States Department of Agriculture, National Oceanic and Atmospheric Administration, National Wildlife Federation, NatureWorks, Elizabeth Nellums, Lyle B. Nichols, Craig Packer, Lucie Penin, The Peregrine Fund, John D. Perrine, Chris Perrins, Serge Planes, Jeremy Potriquet, The Reptile Database, Julia L. Riley, C. Ross, San Diego Zoo, Savannah River Ecology Laboratory/University of Georgia, Sea Turtle Conservancy, Hannah Schardt, J.M. Setchell, Jamie Seymour, Bryan Shorrocks, Emilie C. Snell-Rood, South African National Parks, Joseph A. E. Stewart, Céline Stievenart, Anna Tarter, James H. Thorne, Paul Tolmé, U.S. Department of the Interior, U.S. Fish and Wildlife Service, United States Census Bureau, United States Coast Guard, University of Adelaide, Julie Vercelloni, Washington Department of Fish and Wildlife, Darryl Wheye, WhoZoo, Naomi Wick, E.J. Wickings, Wild Cat Conservation, Wildlife Conservation Network, Ted Williams, J.D. Willson, James B. Wood, World Animal Foundation, David H. Wright, and Brigette Zacharczenko

PHOTO CREDITS

The author would like to thank the following photographers for their creative contributions.

From the National Wildlife Federation Photography Archives:

Matthew Balnis (page 51-top), Debra Botellio (page 14-top left), Hermann Brehm (pages 28 and 50-top), William Brizee (page 58-top), Daniel Brown (page 51-middle), Bob Chauncey (page 27-top), Lynn Cleveland (page 27-bottom), William Crapo (page 53-bottom right), Donna Dannen (page 61-bottom left), Barbaralynne D'Arpino (page 37-bottom right), Jim Duckworth (page 55-top), Josh Edelson (front cover-top left and page 59-middle right), Dick Forehand (page 72-bottom), Richard Greening (page 62-top), Peter Hemming (page 15-top), Susy Horowitz (page 60-top), Arthur Jacoby (page 54-middle), Joao Paulo Krajewski (front cover-top right and page 11-top), Rachel Lewis (page 11-top), Mary Lindhjem (front cover-bottom right and page 74-bottom), Kevin McCarthy (page 15-bottom), Jack McDermott (page 63), Robert Palmer (back cover-bottom and page 75-top), Kim Phillips (page 74-top), Shirley R. Richardson (page 71-bottom right), Joseph Scaringe (page 24-top right), Robin Schall (page 73-top), Howard Sheridan (page 31), Angela Smith (page 13-top right), Janice Sommerville (page 68), Jadwiga-Tabaka (page 56-top), John van Eeden (page 75-bottom), Alex Varani (page 38-bottom), Wade Walcher (page 10-bottom), Garry Walter (46-left), John E Walters (page 52-top), and J. L. Wooden (page 29-bottom)

From Shutterstock:

1082492116 (page 67-top), Sharon Alexander (page 47-top), Juan G. Aunion (page 25-bottom right), Evgeniy Ayupov (page 24-top left), Bonnie Taylor Barry (page 47-bottom), Miles Boyer (page 36-top), Willyam Bradberry (page 57-bottom), Kim Briers (page 64-bottom), Jeremy Brown (page 38-top), Sascha Burkard (page 71-bottom left), Neil Burton (page 21-bottom), Katarina Christenson (page 37-bottom left), Chungking (page 65-top), Ethan Daniels (page 64-top), Darrenp (page 18-bottom), Sam D'Cruz (page 13-bottom), Zacarias Pereira da Mata (page 30-bottom), Michiel de Wit (page 53-bottom left), Rusty Dodson (pages 41-bottom and 33-bottom left), Dennis W. Donohue (page 69-top), EcoPrint (page 25-top), Dirk Ercken (pages 19-bottom and 53-top right), John C. Evans (page 42-bottom), Melinda Fawver (page 36-bottom left), Iakov Filimonov (pages 58-bottom right and 66-bottom), Fivespots (page 32-top), Steffen Foerster (pages 12 and 30-top), Hedrus (page 26 (bottom), Gina Hendrick (pages 3 and 54-top), Parmoht Hongtong (page 35-middle), Eduard Ionescu (page 35-bottom), IrinaK (pages 33-bottom right and 59 top-left), Eric Isselee (page 37-top and middle left), Ammit Jack (page 20-bottom), Rosa Jay (pages 56-bottom and 59-top right and bottom right), Jeep2499 (page 59-middle left), Matt Jeppson (page 32-bottom), JPL Designs (page 45-bottom), Andreas Juergensmeier (page 26-top right), Kagai19927 (page 29-top), Kurt_G (page 37-top right), Ivan Kuzmin (page 45-top), Michelle Lalancette (page 69-bottom), Henrik Larsson (page 35-top), LehaKoK (page 67-bottom), LeonP (page 26-top left), J.Y. Loke (page 19-top), M. Lorenz (page 51-bottom), Julie Lubick (page 62-bottom), Alfredo Maiquez (page 43-top), R. Gino Santa Maria (page 16), Matt9122 (front cover-bottom left and page 10-top), Jason Mintzer (page 13-middle,) Fabien Monteil (page 36-bottom right), Neelsky (page 21-top), Nagel Photography (pages 23-top left, 55-bottom, and 58-bottom left), Alexander M. Omelko (page 25-bottom left), Sari O'Neal (page 33-top), David Osborn (page 23), Pyma (page 34), Yusran Abdul Rahman (page 17), David Rasmus (page 20-top), Morley Read (pages19-middle and 41-top), Reptiles4all (page 24-bottom), Nicky Rhodes (page 52-bottom), Tom Reichner (page 61-bottom right), Steve Schlaeger (page 72-top), Susan Schmitz (page 18-top), Scubaluna (page 39-bottom), Shane Myers Photography (page 61-top), Debbie Steinhausser (page 70), Super Prin (page 46-right), Karen Swanepoel (page 14-middle), Talvi (page 14-bottom), Tania Thomson (pages 48, 49, and 54-bottom), Sergey Uryadnikov (back cover-top and pages 8 and 22), Kristina Vackova (page 39-top), Paul Vinten (page 40-top and bottom), Vaclav Volrab (page 23-bottom), Volt Collection (page 71-top), Pablo Jacinto Yoder (page 43-bottom), Worlds Wildlife Wonders (page 44), and Michael Woodruff (page 42-top)

Other:

United States Fish and Wildlife Service (front jacket flap and pages 60-bottom, 73-bottom, and 77)

INDEX